T0194851

CORPORATE
MISSIONARY

KIANA WHEELER

WESTBOW
PRESS®
A DIVISION OF THOMAS NELSON
& ZONDERVAN

WestBow Press books may be ordered through booksellers or by contacting:

WestBow Press
A Division of Thomas Nelson & Zondervan
1663 Liberty Drive
Bloomington, IN 47403
www.westbowpress.com
1 (866) 928-1240

ISBN: 978-1-9736-7242-5 (sc)
ISBN: 978-1-9736-7243-2 (hc)
ISBN: 978-1-9736-7241-8 (e)

Library of Congress Control Number: 2019912177

Print information available on the last page.

WestBow Press rev. date: 5/28/2020

Contents

Introduction

In the spring of 2017, my husband and I traveled to go on a mission trip. As we were flying back home, I heard God whisper the idea for this book. At the moment, I thought that writing a book sounded like a great adventure and a cool idea. But doubt quickly set in as we landed in our hometown. I became scared of what other people would think if I started writing a book and pursuing the dreams that God gave me.

Fast forward a few months later and I barely wanted to write the book. I allowed the enemy to distract me with the thoughts I mentioned earlier. Even though I knowingly disobeyed God and hadn't started writing the book, I felt as though my career was headed in the right direction as I accepted a new position. However, two weeks after starting the new job, I was rushed to the hospital. I couldn't feel the right side of my face and my right arm went numb. I was shocked to be there and had no preexisting conditions to put me there either. The last time I was in the hospital was when I was being born. But God spoke and ensured I would be 100% healed. I decided to trust him instead of worry. This is where I wrote the first outline of the book, in the hospital bed. In addition to writing the book, I used the time in the hospital to pray for loved ones, nurses, doctors and anyone who came to mind. I even held bible studies with some of the women I was discipling. It was a refreshing time for me and my faith grew tremendously. After 21 days in the hospital I was miraculously healed. My doctors were amazed and called my case a medical mystery.

I've lived most of my Christian life on the sidelines choosing to watch those I saw called to ministry, minister to the lost and pursue their God-given calling. Don't get me wrong I eagerly desire to see the lost come to know Jesus Christ as their Lord and Savior. I never thought I could be effective just by sharing my experience with Jesus. Well that was a complete lie from the devil and I bought into his strategic marketing campaign for years. It's like he was using my personal data to push a tailored message of "you can't do it" everywhere I looked.

As I think back, during college I worked full-time and this is where I began to buy into the call of sharing the gospel with my colleagues. Even though I struggled with self-doubt about how effective I would be. Nevertheless God opened my heart for the people around me who didn't have a relationship with him. This passion to share the gospel was a direct result of God giving me a fresh start through my confession of faith in Jesus. I looked at that as my opportunity to live a redeemed life and seek after Him with all my heart, mind and soul. As I worked full-time in college I started to see the fruit from building a foundation on God not my career aspirations.

God taught me how to listen to my colleagues and to respect where they were spiritually, as a believer or nonbeliever. He taught me how to build authentic relationships, getting to know them as best as possible. I began to develop a mind to pray on their behalf whether for their salvation, to strengthen their walk with Christ, for a sick child, you name it. To this day, God is still calling me to pursue his purpose at work.

The goal of this book is for you to walk away equipped and empowered to reach your colleagues for God. I'm so thankful God asked me to share what my journey has been becoming a *Corporate Missionary*. The stories that I share are my personal testimonies of how God used me at work. Be encouraged as you read because God has something for you to learn and he wants to use you too.

May God open your eyes to see those who are lost around you and may he open your heart to love them. May you grow in Christlikeness and be God's ambassador to win your colleagues back to him. For his glory. Amen.

Kiana Wheeler

Acknowledgements

I'd like to thank my family for being loving and encouraging through this book writing journey.

Thank you to my friends for encouraging me to finish strong. You all were supportive, loving and prayerful.

A very special thank you goes to my amazing husband, Matt. Honey we did this together! I'm forever grateful for your love, support, editing skills and sacrifice to help me see this book to the finish line. You are exactly what your name means, a gift from God, to me. I will love you forever and always.

Chapter 1:

IMPLEMENTING GOD'S EXPECTATIONS

All throughout the New Testament we read how Jesus lived his life. Selfless, patient and sinless all come to mind. He is our great example of how to live our lives. Yet after his resurrection we find a bold call to action in Matthew 28:19-20.

> "Therefore go and make disciples of all nations, baptizing them in the name of the Father and of the Son and of the Holy Spirit, and teaching them to obey everything I have commanded you. And surely I am with you always, to the very end of the age."

In this passages Jesus tells his disciples to go and make new disciples, everywhere. It's one of the first commands he gives after his resurrection. He could have said anything but he said this. I often think about why he gave this commission instead of literally anything else. But I always leave this question with the thought that it had to be this. God wanted to build a relationship with all of humanity and the first disciples were given a part to play in making that happen. I believe though, God used

Jesus to encourage but also to get the point across that - this hope they felt by seeing Jesus alive is the same hope he wanted every human to know and trust in. Jesus lays the foundation of what God expected post-resurrection. From what we see in other books of the New Testament the disciples took this Great Commission to heart and acted quickly.

So do these expectations still hold up today? I'd say yes they do. Most of us know someone who's gone on a mission trip to share the gospel. So we know people are still living to uphold the Great Commission. But does this commission extend to all areas of our lives? Like at work.

In the context of work and the Great Commission, what is God's expectation? Lucky for us we don't have to guess, we have the bible. God has shared his vision for us as well as his expectations. The first expectation is to be imitators of Him, second to walk in love and third to share the gospel.

When it comes to our careers we often have a vision of what it should look like, separate from God's input. However, no matter what we may be striving for at work one of our goals as believers should be to live up to God's expectations. Living up to his expectations solely rests on us stepping out in faith and relying on his strength to live each day for him at work.

Expectation #1 To Be Imitators of God

Growing up I always wanted to do everything my dad did. I loved spending time with him and still do! As I got older, I started noticing that my extended family would often say, "You act just like your dad" or "You can tell that's Erving's child". To me that was a huge compliment because my dad is awesome. He's thoughtful and loves to make sure everyone is having a good time. I was an imitator of my dad; I copied all his actions and those who I walked closely with could pick up on it. It's the same thing with God. We imitate him by embodying his character, actions and behavior. It's that simple. One of my favorite characteristics of God is that he is love and displays his love to us by being gracious and merciful when we don't deserve it. The purpose of this book is to encourage you to share the gospel with your colleagues. For some of you this might be a huge step out of your comfort zone. But there is hope and you can be an imitator of God on your job which will help you reach your colleagues.

You can imitate God on your job by extending grace to colleagues even when you don't think they deserve it. We need God's grace otherwise we'd be left to make atonement for our sins and the only way to pay for that would be to die for our own sins. God had a plan though, and came to our rescue by sacrificing his perfect and blameless son, Jesus. He died for our sins even though we didn't deserve it. That's called grace! Every last person makes mistakes not just our colleagues but us too. We all need second chances and God gave us that when he sent his son.

Romans 8: 3-4 states "The law of Moses was unable to save us because of the weakness of our sinful nature. So, God did what the law could not do. He sent his own Son in a body like the body's we sinners have. And in that body God declared an end to sin's control over us by giving his Son as a sacrifice for our sins. He did this so that the just requirement of the law would be fully satisfied for us, who no longer follow our sinful nature but instead follow the Spirit."

Because of this believers should know what it means to have second chances. This is one of God's expectations of us as we seek to be imitators of him on our jobs.

Expectation #2 To Walk in Love

When I think about what it means to walk in love, I envision Christ carrying his cross on the way to his crucifixion. He walked knowing he was going to die. I imagine the love he carried in his heart. I also imagine that he must have thought long and hard, knowing he was the only sacrifice to make things right between us and God. He was perfect but still took on the burden of our sin. But even though he was crucified, he didn't stay dead. Jesus rose from the grave and proved he was the son of God. His death meant life for anyone who believed and confessed that he was the Son of God and both Lord and Savior. Romans 8:5 says, "But God clearly shows and proves His own love for us, by the fact that while we were still sinners, Christ died for us."

His sacrifice was the key to our freedom from sin. The sacrificial way Jesus expressed his love for us is foremost what gave us salvation but also an example of the way we are to live for the sake of others. Now we, as believers, can learn to love others like Jesus loves us sacrificially, even when it inconveniences us.

That is the type of love that wins over our colleagues who do not have a relationship with Him.

God lays the perfect practical example in Mark 12:30, "...And you shall love the Lord your God with all your heart, and with all your soul, and with all your mind, and with all your strength." God maps out a fourfold love which points us to the significance that total devotion is demanded. Our soul is our heart, it's our mental power, emotional power and will power. Our soul influences how we react, think and do things. When we allow the Lord to save our soul, we're handing over everything that makes us, us. Proverbs 4:23 says, "Above all else, guard your heart, for everything you do flows from it." Your thoughts and emotions will determine your decisions and they start in your heart. Are your thoughts and emotions in line with God's character? In what ways have you displayed God's love recently on your job? These are the types of questions to keep in mind as you think about God's expectations.

God expects us to walk in love by first loving him then we learn to stand guard against the wicked desires of our hearts and seek to pursue God's heart above all else. By doing so, we lay the foundation of becoming effective witnesses in the corporate world and see real growth with our colleagues.

Walking in love was hard for me to truly grasp because it involved being vulnerable and I've only just learned how. I've always been a friendly person. I can talk to anyone and make strong connections but walking in love was not as evident as I had thought. It was the small things that led me to see the truth. I had to allow the Holy Spirit to change my mindset which changed my actions. I had to renew my mind daily. For example, I'd prioritize getting to know my colleagues by connecting over lunch and even spending time with them outside of work. However, these get-to-know-you moments were just another Christian-y to-do list item for me. I didn't approach them with the heart of Jesus, meaning I wasn't getting to know them, because I was listening to speak, not listening to understand. To say it plainly, it was a task, assigned by my legalistic mindset of how I thought God wanted me to engage them. I mean didn't Jesus have all those meals with people to get to know them and share the truth about the Kingdom of God? And to answer my own question, yes, but he walked in love with the purest intentions of just loving them. It wasn't anything anyone said that made me realize all of this. It was time spent with Jesus during my morning devotions that opened my eyes to see my colleagues as humans who did not know God, not as a project. They needed to see Him through me by way of acts of kindness, displaying patience, exuding joy, listening to understand and most importantly love.

I started to pivot my approach, still connecting over lunch but also loving them right where they were without the feeling of checking them off my spiritual to-do list. I could tell my efforts made a difference because they were vulnerable and truthful with the little things in their life. That's what walking in love is all about, not making your colleagues feel like they're on your "Christian-y get to know you - to see instant results" list. But just loving people where they are at and speaking the truth along the way. It's the Holy Spirit's job to change their hearts, we are just his loving messengers.

Expectation #3 Share the Gospel

God expects us to share the gospel. Point. Blank. Period.

All throughout the bible we find stories about God sending people to share His message, either to a person, a family or a nation. For example, there was the prophet Samuel (1 Samuel 7) who was sent to the people of Israel telling them to seek God and repent. Then there was Jonah (Jonah 1:2) who was sent by God to share His message in Nineveh. Finally, and most importantly there was Jesus. Jesus was sent to proclaim the good news of salvation and to encourage Israel to turn from their sins, believe and follow him.

If we look closely, we'll see that Jesus was an expert teacher of the scriptures and was able to interpret them giving insight that wasn't yet heard. He always prioritized sharing the good news of salvation through repentance wherever he went. He perfected living according to God's expectations.

How do you prioritize sharing the gospel at work?

If you weren't able to answer the question above, here is some fuel to help ignite your desire to share the gospel. In my opinion, Romans 10:14 can be the most encouraging and convicting scripture as it relates to sharing the gospel. It states,

> *"How then can they call on the one they have not believed in? And how can they believe in the one of whom they have not heard? And how can they hear without someone preaching to them?"*

Paul's appeal to us through this scripture is simple. He's saying don't just be a nice good Christian and never utter the name of Jesus or how he's changed your life. And then turnaround and expect your colleagues will come to know and accept Jesus Christ as their Lord and Savior. That type of shallow expectation doesn't produce a harvest. If anything, it produces a lot of good intentions that rarely get acted upon.

I remember when I first started working for Marriott. I had already received Jesus as my Lord and Savior but was very afraid to share my faith with my colleagues. I believe I was around 21 years old and was on my last stretch in college. My major was Hospitality Management, so working at Marriott was a big deal! It was such a big deal, I didn't want to jeopardize my relationships at work by sharing how God changed my life. I'd often say to myself, "Just invite them for an Easter or Christmas service." Even now as I write this I am cringing because I had no hope for my colleagues nor confidence that God could use me to reach them.

One day at work it was announced that we would have new interns for a full calendar year. I was excited to meet our new employees who were coming from all over the world. After a few months of getting to know one of the interns from Ukraine, I felt the Holy Spirit nudge me to ask if she believed in God. From that one question it opened future conversations for me to ask more questions about her thoughts on humanity, good vs. evil and faith. I was shocked! I finally had the courage to share the gospel with her. Stepping out on faith, I invited my colleague to attend a Sunday service and to my surprise she accepted. It was the first time I invited anyone from my job to church and not just think about it. I can't remember the message that Sunday, but I do remember she mentioned how much she really enjoyed the service and had never experienced a church message like the one we heard. I was amazed and even now, I look back at the pictures from that Sunday and see me, a young girl wanting so desperately to be used by God not just to share the gospel but to make disciples as well.

Can You Make The Time?

It's so easy to allow our work to demand how our time is spent on the job. But I challenge you to look beyond the work that you do day-to-day and seek to "insert Jesus" in your everyday work conversations. I've experienced that when I developed relationships with my colleagues, whether in a group setting or one on one, God shows me through his Holy Spirit who he's leading me to build a deeper relationship with. Over time I have become accustomed to how God wants to work through me on my job.

And please do not let these simple words lead you to believe that the process was easy or is easy for that matter. You may be thinking to yourself, "How can I do this?" "Do I even hear from the Holy Spirit clearly?" "I'm just trying to work on my relationship with Jesus before I go out and share the gospel with my colleagues." Trust me, I've been there and at times I'm still there! Life as a Christian can be hard but God will give us the strength and wisdom to accomplish his will even in difficult circumstances. He is the master teacher and we have the privilege to learn from him. Let's look at the first disciples. According to the culture at the time, disciples were to follow a Rabbi and study underneath his leadership for at least 15 years before they were able to teach others. However, we see a different story unfold with Jesus and his disciples. He taught them in less time than the culture would have approved and then sent them out to reach the lost. Don't you think God can do the same for us? It's only a matter of being willing to humble ourselves and learn.

Charles Stanley was once quoted saying, "God's plan for enlarging His kingdom is so simple - one person telling another about the Savior. Yet we're busy and full of excuses. Just remember, someone's eternal destiny is at stake. The joy you'll have when you meet that person in heaven will far exceed any discomfort you felt in sharing the gospel."

This encourages me because whenever I want to shy away from a "God conversation", I'm reminded of how these small interactions have an eternal impact.

The Declaration Every Believer Can Make

Today I said the United States pledge of allegiance. It's been a few years since I've attended an event where I had to say it. But it reminded me of how we as followers of Christ pledge allegiance to God, first, foremost and above all else.

I pledge allegiance to the Flag of the United States of America

and to the Republic for which it stands,

one Nation under God, indivisible,

with liberty and justice for all.

Think of the significance of reciting the Pledge of Allegiance. As United States citizens we are promising to be true to our country and the states that have joined to make our country. We are stating that we are a republic, which is a country where the people choose their representatives to make laws for them, that is the government of the people. And we are one single nation under God's authority and that nation cannot be split into parts. Lastly, we are declaring freedom and fairness for each person in the country.

Similarly, there are many parallels with our pledge of allegiance to God. We too are making a bold stand to uphold the standards of his kingdom. If I had to create a pledge of allegiance for Christians it would say, "I pledge allegiance to God and his holy word. I will make it a lamp unto my feet and a light unto my path. For his kingdom I will stand firm and go to every nation to proclaim the good news of Jesus Christ in love and humility."

Our allegiance to God is our confession of faith, it's our sounding board for moments in life when we are challenged with conflicting priorities. It helps us stay on the narrow path when the world tells us to break our allegiance and become traitors of God's kingdom. In my personal relationship with

God, I've learned that in order to be successful in the corporate world, I had to know my identity was rooted in him. Part of this journey included daily declarations that reaffirmed my allegiance to God. This exercise was great. I felt this sense of "heck yeah, I'm going to be a great corporate missionary for God!" But then, there were moments when I would wake up and remember how a colleague treated me the day before. Or even worse, how I missed the mark by not showing grace and my whole morning would be thrown off. But I was relentless in my pursuit of God and by his grace I was able to state these declarations even though I didn't always feel like it.

My favorite morning declaration comes from Ephesians 2:8-10 NIV, it states, "For it is by grace you have been saved, through faith – and this is not from yourselves, it is the gift of God – not by works, so that no one can boast. For we are God's handiwork, created in Christ Jesus to do good works, which God prepared in advance for us to do."

This declaration just sets the tone for me. When we state this aloud, we are declaring that our salvation from God's wrath, because of our sinfulness, is His gracious gift to us through our faith in Jesus Christ. We cannot earn salvation by doing "works" whether through trying to execute the law perfectly or trying to make many disciples as a corporate missionary. Nope! Such a legalistic approach is discouraged throughout scripture. If you could earn your salvation, you wouldn't need Jesus. God knew we could never be good enough on our own to meet his holy standard. That's why we need Jesus.

The second part of this scripture that I love to declare is that

I am God's masterpiece, created to do good works. He has a sovereign purpose and plan for all of us that he prepared before we were even born. God is a creator; he can do this, create a specific purpose for each one of us to accomplish and pursue.

After you've realized that you can't work your way to getting saved because it's a free gift from God, then you can freely set out to do the good works he has prepared for you in advance. It's a mind shift. Good works can look like sharing the gospel of Christ with your colleagues, business partners, or whomever God leads you to. Good works are demonstrated in gratitude, character and actions. They are the fruit of our salvation, not the cause of it. Out of a heart of gratitude to God for his salvation our life goal should include wanting to share this new-found hope with everyone we know.

God is Not Looking at Your Human Credentials But at Your Heart and Willingness to Obey

In the book of 1 Samuel, Saul, who was from the Israelite tribe of Benjamin, was looking for his father's lost donkeys. Unable to find them he took one of his servants and set out to speak with Samuel the prophet to ask which direction the donkeys might have gone (1 Samuel 9:6). Prior to Saul's journey to find Samuel, God instructed Samuel to appoint the first king of Israel. God shared with him who the king would be and that he would come from the tribe of Benjamin (1 Samuel 9:16). The bible states that Saul was a handsome young man who was a head taller than anyone else. After meeting the prophet Samuel, Saul, had an encounter with God that changed his heart (1 Samuel 10:9).

What I find interesting about this story is the power of God that was displayed in Saul's life. He had the looks and stature of a king, but God wasn't impressed by that. He wanted Saul's heart to display the character of God in order to lead the people. Hopefully this is encouraging as you seek to be missionaries on your jobs. Some of you may have three degrees, two assistants and an executive level position. Others might be finishing your evening MBA program or you may very well be someone's assistant. God doesn't care what title or position you hold, he is looking at your heart. The best ability you can have is your availability. God is looking for men and women who will make themselves available to share the gospel with their colleagues. It starts with a heart submitted to do God's will, regardless of your title.

As I'm writing this book I am currently working as an executive assistant. However, when God first started talking to me about writing this book, I was in a leadership role for a national television network. Because I had the lofty title at the network, I felt I had the credentials to make a difference for God in the workplace. I was already beginning to see some fruit from sharing the gospel but God soon showed me that my title isn't what qualified me for his work. My position ended abruptly, I was forced to look for another job. So I took an opportunity as an executive assistant for a small non-profit.

What was a seemingly small level of influence with my new job because of my title became my greatest season as a corporate missionary. I began to see God reveal himself to my colleagues through my one-on-one conversations. I'm thankful God placed me in this season. I've learned that he just wants someone who is available to follow his lead no matter who you are.

My first few months as an executive assistant were humbling. I went from being a strategic thinker in my previous job to just taking orders from others. One day our small team hired additional help. Our first hire was a recent college graduate and was eager to learn her new role. I was tasked with onboarding and helping her get started. We spent the first three weeks together every day reviewing campaigns, donor lists and memorizing the elected officials in our area. Spending that much time together allowed us to get to know each other quickly. By the fourth week it was time for her to start leading some of her projects with minimal supervision. She was off to a great start.

A few months had passed, and she was leading the meetings for our committees and was given a new project. We soon found she was having difficulty leading this project on her own. She quickly went from being favored by leadership to becoming an outcast almost overnight. It was a very difficult situation to watch. Our leader would yell and belittle her instead of coaching her through the project. As I watched all of this unfold, I prayed often and listened for God's instructions. Then it came. God spoke. God wanted me to use the relationship that I built with her to engage in a conversation about faith.

One day I invited her to go on a walk to get ice cream. While on our walk I asked her how she felt about the job and how she wanted things to move forward. I listened intently as she shared how she was hurt by the comments from leadership. They had called her a disappointment. As she continued to share, I listened and heard how broken she felt. She talked about how she didn't know her purpose since graduating college and talked about what her parents wanted her to do. At that moment I saw an open door and asked if she believed in God. She said she believed in a higher power. I asked how she would describe God/the higher power and she replied. That led into another question where I asked what she thought God expected of us and then I asked her how she would rate herself on meeting those expectations.

Her replies to these questions opened the door for me to share my faith and talk about how I find purpose through having a relationship with God. I shared that my peace and joy is rooted in God and I had the choice to respond according to my faith or my frustration. She chimed in that she wanted peace in her life. I took that as an opportunity to share the gospel. Sharing that through the confession of her faith that Jesus is Lord and did raise from the dead she would have eternal life. And that subsequently she would have peace and many other wonderful benefits. I highlighted that change won't happen through trying harder but only through encountering the radical grace of God.

That same month God opened my eyes to another opportunity with the same colleague. This time it was around the holidays and we were the only two in the office. By this time, we had built a solid relationship at work and were texting each other funny memes on the weekends. We had become friends. We were sitting eating lunch together and the conversation led us to talk about our families and holiday traditions. She shared that her parents split up while she was young and because of this she doesn't have much of a relationship with her dad.

We talked about how that affected her view of God and she replied that sometimes she doesn't think God cares about her. We talked through her thoughts, and I shared my story of how God stepped in as my heavenly father once I put my faith in Jesus. In my mind I kept telling myself to stop sharing and that none of this would make sense to her. But it did. God used me to connect the dots for her. Showing how he wanted to be her heavenly father, guide her in life and express the unconditional love she desired. In that moment, I asked if she wanted to accept Jesus as her Lord and Savior and be connected to her heavenly father. She was ready and I could sense it. I felt God's presence in that room, I'll never forget it. But that day she replied she wanted to think about it. I took it as an opportunity to invite her to church and continue to build a relationship because I could see God was stirring up some things inside of her.

Through this role as an executive assistant, God changed my perspective to see that titles and credentials do not matter. Think of it this way, if God chose us by our credentials or platform then that would mean we are using our own natural strength to obtain favor with God. So those who may be uneducated or lower on the career chain wouldn't catch God's attention to do his work. This is not true! Romans 2:11 NIV teaches us that, "God does not show favoritism." Yes, you read that right. God loves us immeasurably but he doesn't show favoritism.

17

Picking up from our story in 1 Samuel, Saul is now crowned king of Israel. As the leader, he was responsible for caring for and leading the people of Israel. In 1 Samuel 13 NIV, Saul starts to abandon this responsibility by choosing to sacrifice instead of obeying God's plan. Israel was under attack by the Philistines and they were outnumbered. Most of the Israelite troops aborted their mission and left Saul. Tragic! Saul had 3,000 personally chosen troops but later in the chapter we discovered only 600 were registered. Saul more than likely started to panic, and this wouldn't have been his first time. Saul was given a message from Samuel to wait 7 days for the appointed time and then further instructions would be available. Saul waited 7 days but instead of waiting for further instructions, he went ahead and offered a burnt offering. This was a job that was to be completed by Samuel, Israel's priest.

Saul missed the message that the Lord's favor didn't come through the sacrifice of the burnt offering but through faithfulness and obedience to his instruction (1 Samuel 15:22 NIV). Because of Saul's impulsive leadership style, he jumped the gun and did not heed the instruction of his advisor, Samuel. The same could happen to us if we are led by our emotions and react in haste instead of following God's instructions. We too could end up failing when God originally had us set up to succeed. God is looking at our heart to obey him.

Saul's job was to lead and care for the people of Israel. The people were expecting him to avenge them as their King. But he needed to trust in the King of Kings, not his title, in order to be successful. Imagine what his testimony would have been like had he trusted in the Lord. He would have learned that obedience to God's instructions brings salvation. The Israelites would have seen his obedience and developed a deeper devotion and reverence for the Lord. Unfortunately, Saul's disobedience ultimately led to him losing his position as king. God eventually sent Samuel, the prophet, to appoint another king from among the Israelites. Someone whose heart was committed to obeying and pleasing God.

What project or situation do you need to trust the Lord with? It could be a difficult assignment or even difficult people. Think about who might be watching you on your job that's not a follower of Jesus. Imagine the outcome of your obedience sparking hope and inspiring your colleagues to ask how you got that project to succeed. Now is the opportunity to have you insert Jesus into your reply and tell them how you trusted the Lord to guide your every step. It's a subtle way to share the gospel through your personal experience with God. Remember God wants to use you, not because of your position but because of your willingness to be obedient and available.

CHAPTER 1 – PRACTICAL APPLICATION

Congratulations, you've completed reading chapter one. Now here's the fun part, applying what you've learned and researching how you can grow and mature in your walk with Christ at work.

In this chapter you read God's expectations; to be imitators of God, to walk in love and to share the gospel of Jesus and make disciples.

Imitators of God

Ephesians 5:1 NASB says, "Therefore be imitators of God, as beloved children;"

The Greek word for imitator is mimētēs (the root of the English term, mimic). It means "one who imitates or emulates" and is "the positive imitation that arises by admiring the pattern set by someone worthy of emulation, i.e. a mentor setting a proper example."

Jesus is our God approved example to imitate and emulate our life after. If we are devoted to God as beloved children, we begin to develop a reverence towards imitating Christ as we learn and admire his perfect and blameless life.

What do you admire about Christ's life?

_____

_____

List two examples based on Christ's life that you can actively imitate and apply to your work life this week?

_____

_____

_____

_____

Reminder: When we imitate God, we are submitting to his Lordship as King and Ruler over our will (mind, thoughts, emotions). In other words, we make a daily decision to lean not on our own understanding BUT acknowledge Him in all our ways (Proverbs 3:5 NIV).

To Walk in Love

Ephesians 5:2 says, "And walk in the way of love, just as Christ loved us..." Walking in love is a direct extension of being an imitator of God. We can learn to love others like Jesus loves us, sacrificially, even when it inconveniences us. That is the type of love that wins over our colleagues who do not have a relationship with Him.

Pray and ask God to show you how-to walk in love on your job. Write, type on your phone or voice record what you hear throughout the day.

Sharing the Gospel

Romans 10:14 NIV states, "How then can they call on the one they have not believed in? And how can they believe in the one of whom they have not heard? And how can they hear without someone preaching to them?" Although these are rhetorical questions, your answer is shown in your desire to insert the gospel into your conversations at work. If the gospel has impacted your life and you are no longer devoted to sin but have been redeemed through Christ and are set free from the power that sin had on you, well then, that's a story to share. Think of it this way, if you had the data and insights to leverage and win a key business account, wouldn't you share it? Comparatively, you do have the insights and data to prove how God changed your life through faith in Christ.

Recall a time when you shared the gospel at work?

_____

_____

_____

_____

_____

If you haven't shared the gospel with a colleague before, what may be holding you back? If you have shared the gospel, how can you go deeper in conversation with this colleague?

_____

_____

_____

_____

_____

_____

Whether you struggle to share the gospel or have done it many times, pray. Ask God to show you who he's leading you to. Then pray and ask for boldness to do it.

Reminder: We must keep praying for boldness whenever we need it. Even Paul, who wrote to the Ephesians, asked them to pray that he "may declare it [the good news of Christ] fearlessly..." (Ephesians 6:20). This request came from a man who shared the gospel numerous times before.

Chapter 2:

GOD'S PURPOSE OVER YOUR PLANNED AGENDA

Your success at work begins with following God's plan. I'd like to shed light on what it can look like when we don't follow God's purpose and instead develop a spirit of arrogance. As an ambassador for Christ, you must fight against the temptation to revel in your reputation, position at work, your work given authority and your intellect. God's purpose for every believer starts with developing our character in him so that when he makes his appeal through us to our colleagues, they'll see him not us.

In 1 Samuel 10 we learn about a man named Saul. He had an encounter with God, received a changed heart and the Spirit of God came powerfully upon him. Then just a few scriptures later, the prophet Samuel summoned the people of Israel to appoint the king. This is where we see a first glimpse of Saul's downward spiral. Instead of coming forward in front of the people of Israel, Saul hid among the supplies. He hesitated to accept God's purpose to announce him as king. God's plan was to give him the responsibility of reigning over the people of Israel and saving them from the power of their enemies. After assuming the throne, Saul continued to hesitate following God's purpose and plan for the monarchy. He made impulsive decisions and promises without God's consent. One time he went as far as making an oath cursing anyone who ate food before evening came, before he had avenged himself on his enemies. The punishment if someone broke this oath was death (1 Samuel 14:24). Then it came time to enforce this oath. However, King Saul's son ate honey before sundown but he didn't have the courage to carry out the punishment (1 Samuel 14:34-45).

We can look to God's word to find that when we follow his purpose, we succeed because our plan becomes aligned with his. In John 15:5-8 Jesus tells us, "I am the vine; you are the branches. If you remain in me and I in you, you will bear much fruit; apart from me you can do nothing. If you do not remain in me, you are like a branch that is thrown away and withers; such branches are picked up, thrown into the fire and burned. If you remain in me and my words remain in you, ask whatever you wish, and it will be done for you. This is to my Father's glory, that you bear much fruit, showing yourselves to be my disciples."

First, how can we ensure we're remaining in God? We'll know by the fruit we're bearing in our life. When we remain in God we should produce fruit because of our priority to stay connected to the life-giving vine. A practical way of staying connected is saying yes to God's plan each day before going to work. That means studying his word and praying his promises over our life and our colleagues. It also means examining ourselves to see if there are any areas in our own lives that we need to submit to God. This could include fear of failure, an apathetic mindset in reaching our colleagues for Christ, or doubting if our colleagues can actually be reached with the gospel.

By taking these initial steps we will begin to bear the fruit of a life transformed by God. We'll start to produce fruit like joy to do God's will at work. Whatever the circumstance we may find ourselves in God's peace will be available to us to keep us steady. We will have patience to wait on God for his direction. To remain in God we will build a godly character that pleases and reveres him as Lord over all areas of our life, including work. It's important to note that when we make it a priority to remain in him we slowly start to remove any expectations of what work should look like according to us. We make room for God's purpose to take over our heart and lead us to walking out his plan of seeing our colleagues brought closer to a relationship with him through us.

Following God's Lead

In Daniel 1, we are introduced to a story about a guy named Daniel. Daniel was recruited for his job in the royal court under Nebuchadnezzar, King of Babylon. He was taken to Babylon with three of his friends and many other young men for a 3 year management rotational program. The program included learning the Babylonian languages, literature and culture. After completing the program, Daniel and his friends were brought before the king. He found none equal to them and so they entered into his service.

Shortly after this Nebuchadnezzar had a dream that caused him great trouble because he could not understand it. He summoned all the magicians, enchanters, sorcerers and astrologers to interpret his dream, but they were unable to do so. The king was so frustrated that no one could help him that he decided to kill all the wise men in Babylon, including Daniel and his friends. Daniel heard about this. He prayed and received revelation from God for the king's dream in a vision. In this crucial first win on the job, all the pagan training that Daniel received proved worthless. Only by God's divine revelation was he able to interpret the dream correctly. Just like Daniel we may be classically trained in marketing, finance, engineering and so on. But God is looking to see if we will seek him and his wisdom for our work-related situations. Daniel chose to seek the Lord and was able to bring discernment because of his work and life being submitted under God's authority. Are you seeking the Lord when your colleagues come to you with their issues? Or are you giving advice that will still leave them searching?

My favorite takeaway from this story is our need to pray, especially when we notice that our colleagues are troubled. We can pray and ask God for divine revelation to understand what is going on in their lives and share his words to encourage them.

One time I had a dream that a colleague of mine was crying at her desk and there was this cloud of gray over her. When I woke up that morning, I prayed and asked God for understanding of the dream and for an opportunity to speak one-on-one with her. God quickly made a way and I happened to run into her on my morning coffee break. With the boldness given to me by the Holy Spirit, I shared with her the dream and she began to weep. I told her God had given me this dream and told me he wanted to be her peace. She shared that her husband had been having an affair and decided to leave her for another woman. She was devastated and I was shocked. At that moment, God gave me a word of encouragement to share and she received it with gratitude. I share this story because if I had been focused on me, I would have missed out on providing a word of encouragement to a colleague who desperately needed to hear from God. The Lord used his spirit to give me boldness to speak and the vision to see the big picture of using this moment to continue building a relationship with her.

While I was on this job, it was the hardest season I faced in my career. I had a colleague that purposely left me off emails, excluding me from information that pertained to me doing my job. On my third day at the job I was pulled into my director's office, for what I thought was to review the next day's onboarding materials. Out of nowhere, this meeting turned into a conversation about me challenging her authority. Third day folks. Most days I felt like an outcast and I quickly began seeing the petty work culture. I doubted my purpose, my talent and if God would avenge me from what seemed like fierce enemies. God showed me a valuable lesson which was to trust him and his process. Many days I felt like I was in a lion's den waiting to be devoured by some of my colleagues. I even called out sick a few times because it was hard to go to work and deal with the culture. But I made a choice to pray. I sought God more than I ever did before and I began to trust that he was going to work all things together for my good. I had a lot of emotionally draining days but I found value in learning to follow God's lead. By making this intentional choice I was able to hear God's voice and use wisdom when it came down to addressing some of my colleagues about their less than welcoming attitudes.

Daniel went through a similar situation but his fierce enemies threw him in an actual lion's den. Daniel was still operating in an official capacity in the kingdom but there was a new king on the throne, King Darius. Darius appointed Daniel as one of three administrators responsible for keeping approximately 40 local rulers accountable as they ruled throughout the kingdom. The role of administrator was also to ensure that the king didn't suffer any loss. Daniel in his new role, was killing it! He did such a great job and distinguished himself by his exceptional qualities that the king planned to set him over the whole kingdom. However his colleagues both the administrators and the local rulers didn't want this to happen. They could not find any corruption in him because he was a trustworthy and honest leader. (Daniel 6:1-5)

When the men realized they would never find any basis for charges against Daniel, they went after his relationship with God. So the administrators and satraps went as a group to the king advising him to issue an edict and enforce the decree that anyone who prays to any god or human being during the next thirty days, unless it is the king, should be thrown into the lion's den. These people were so petty. They traveled as a group and found Daniel praying and asking God for help. They immediately went to the king and shared what they saw. The king was in such distress because he knew he had to carry out the punishment. Daniel was thrown into the lion's den but God sent an angel to protect him and closed the mouth of the lions. When the king came to check on Daniel he found him unharmed and was amazed. Daniel shared that he was found innocent in God's sight, nor had he ever done any wrong before the king. He was lifted out the lion's den and was restored to his rightful place in the kingdom and continued to find favor with the king. At the end, the king issued a decree that in every part of his kingdom people must fear and reverence the God of Daniel. Wow!

We can learn to follow God's lead by first not wavering in our devotion to him. Just like Daniel, I was in a really bad work environment at the company I mentioned earlier. But I continued to devote myself to God. I focused on doing my job well and using my platform as a leader to share my testimony with anyone God directed me to. I received favor with people that only God could orchestrate because of my willingness to follow his lead even in the midst of persecution. I say all this to say that this job was not easy, nor was Daniel's, but we did not let our circumstances take our focus off God's plan to use us at work. This can also be true for you and it will start with following God's lead no matter what you're faced with. On this job, I saw two people come to experience God as their heavenly father, not just as a religious figure that they happened to pray to when things got rough. Let this be your motivation to keep following God's lead in all areas of your life especially your work.

But Are You Consistent and Persevering?

Let's be honest, God will sometimes ask us to stay at a job that we can't stand. He'll ask us to trust him and lean not on our own understanding but in all our ways acknowledge him and he will make our paths straight. When God calls us to stay, we have to realize that he has something for us to experience that this company or position can teach us. If we leave prematurely, we forfeit developing consistency, perseverance and faithfulness for doing what God has asked. Essentially we are choosing to abide in our own character instead of developing godly character.

Psalms 46:10 NIV reminds us to, "...Be still, and know that I am God." Say what? Be still? Yes, be still. If you work in a corporate setting, you more than likely have not developed this skill. Let's be real. Especially if you are in Sales, Marketing, Customer Service or Human Resources. We apply for opportunities that tell us we must be good at multitasking and know how to work in a fast-paced environment. But spiritually do we know how to be still? This means do we know how to wait patiently while God maps out the next step without us giving our input or complaining. By embracing this command we build up a tolerance of being consistent to do what God is telling us to do. Being still means to let go and let God fight our battles. It means allowing him to open the hearts of our colleagues to receive Jesus as their Lord and Savior. And whatever else we need from him that doesn't involve us trying to make things happen. Being still means persevering through prayer when things don't line up at work. This process doesn't have to decrease our zeal for doing the will of God on our job. But we can have a surge of enthusiasm by trusting God's ability to make things happen, not our own.

Chapter 2 – Practical Application

Choosing God's purpose over your planned agenda is an intentional step that happens every day of our life. When we make a decision to submit to His Lordship in our career, we are choosing to abide in Him. What else qualifies as remaining in Christ?

In John 15:5-8 we see Jesus saying, "Remain in me" multiple times. The repetition in this passage gives emphasis to the fact that living in unity with Christ is absolutely necessary. In order to answer the question above you must ask yourself a few more questions to come to terms with the truth.

A. Am I chasing a shiny new toy? Is the shiny new toy in line with God's purpose for my life/career?

B. Am I praying to God and asking for his wisdom on big and small matters?

C. Am I listening for his instruction to guide me?

D. Am I pursuing the thing that will bring God glory?

Have you answered the questions above? Are there any other questions that you can ask yourself to identify if you're abiding in Christ? Feel free to take a few minutes to really talk this out with yourself. It's so important to be honest with yourself to assess where you're at.

Looking back at the passage, verse 7 says, "If you remain in me and my words remain in you, ask whatever you wish, and it will be done for you." It is impossible to pray correctly apart from knowing and believing in the teaching of Christ. God's word is the strategic plan for the rest of our lives and without spending daily intentional time in His word we shortcut ourselves from having a career that bears fruit and brings glory to God. In John 14:26 NIV it says, "the Holy Spirit is a Helper, whom the Father will send in My name, He will teach you all things, and bring to your remembrance all that I said to you." This means the Holy Spirit can only bring to your remembrance what you have read or been exposed to about God. I take this scripture and use it to fuel my desire to read and study God's word every day.

What practical steps have you taken to remain in Christ?

_____

_____

_____

_____

_____

Have you made an intentional choice to pursue God's purpose for your career? Yes or No. What does the next step look like for you to pursue God's purpose?

_____

_____

_____

_____

_____

_____

_____

Chapter 3:

Resolving Conflict According To God's Instruction

Let's be honest, corporate life can be stressful especially with all the responsibilities, meetings and meetings for the meetings. The culture of an organization is an important factor that can affect your stress level. Although I'm talking about the organization as a whole, for some of you the most stressful part of work can be the people that you work with. By now you should already know that I am pushing for you to be a bold sharer of the gospel of Jesus. But I'm no dummy, I know that conflict in the workplace is real and can be the very thing standing in the way of you developing relationships with your colleagues and sharing the gospel. Trust me I've been there.

In His infinite wisdom, God has asked that we love the unlovable and to be reconcilers. As a believer, we often forget that we were once at odds with God because of our sin. Our relationship with him was fragmented and broken because of our sinful actions. However, what we read over and over again in the bible is that God desired to be in relationship with mankind and his response to our act of war was love. He pursued us with love and the opportunity for reconciliation through our faith in Jesus Christ. Think about the great lengths that God took to bring reconciliation to us. He sent his son, Jesus, to live a perfect life all while experiencing the same situations we face. Then he died a sinner's death that he did not deserve. Jesus Christ was perfect and without blame. His sacrifice gave all of us a clear path to reconciliation with God if we put our faith in him. Oh, and not to forget, Jesus rose on the third day proving he was the Son of God and he still lives today. God pursues us with love even though he was mistreated by us. We can follow his example in work-related conflicts.

If we can't get over being offended, let down, or even persecuted by colleagues then we'll fail miserably at making an impact at work. We'll try to do this gospel sharing thing on our own strength all while trying to fight through the pain, frustration and disappointment. It's likely we won't come across as genuine and trust me, our colleagues can sense that a mile away. But amid hurt feelings, offense, and even persecution the Lord has called us to be reconcilers.

The Ministry of Reconciliation

2 Corinthians 5:18-20 NIV states, "All this is from God, who reconciled us to himself through Christ and gave us the ministry of reconciliation, that God was reconciling the world to himself in Christ, not counting people's sins against them. And he has committed to us the message of reconciliation. We are therefore Christ's ambassadors, as though God were making his appeal through us."

This passage shows that God's intention wasn't for us to be reconciled to him and then go about our way. It extended to us being his ambassadors, at work, as He makes his appeal through us to our colleagues.

I have struggled with the idea of being an ambassador for Christ. I have never been afraid of talking about God and faith in the workplace. However, I had a narrow view of who I thought God wanted me to engage with. Most days, I engaged with the colleagues who were easiest to talk to. My colleagues who were difficult made me cringe at the thought of trying to ask them anything outside of work-related topics. But the Holy Spirit kept nudging me to submit my thoughts for God's thoughts about my colleagues. After all, they are his creation too and he wants to have a relationship with them. Once again prayer played a significant role as I learned to be a true ambassador for Christ. I often prayed for boldness. But mostly for the opportunity to share the gospel with my colleagues who were difficult, even if I knew there was a chance I would be rejected.

Shortly after graduating college I landed a job in a luxury hotel. When I started the job there wasn't a formal on-boarding period so I learned the role as I did it. After a few weeks I noticed one of the leaders would belittle me in front of the team. At first I brushed it off because I knew that in order to succeed I would need this leader to help me grow and learn the business. However, this difficult leader seemed to find ways to stunt my growth. There were many situations when I was given just enough information to do my job but not enough to grow and expand my understanding. It was tough working with this difficult leader. I felt like a failure and as if I didn't fit in. All while having these thoughts and feelings I still prayed that God would give me boldness and opportunities to share the gospel. But in my heart I was ready to leave this job.

As time went by, I started to learn the culture and made good working relationships with my peers and the other leaders. After some time on the job I was promoted with more leadership responsibilities and had to begin working closely with the difficult leader. I quickly changed my prayers from asking for boldness to asking for God's love to be displayed through me. Every day I reminded myself to be slow to speak and quick to listen. I was still at a place in my walk where I probably would have allowed pettiness to rise up in me if I wasn't walking in the Spirit. Through it all God began to show me my heart towards this difficult leader. I was just as much a part of the problem as they were, simply because I had not loved this difficult leader in my heart. God in his graciousness towards me helped me to heal. Even though I was successful and worked through my issues the best I could, I still had an underlying attitude of not wanting to be bothered by God to engage this difficult leader.

Towards the end of my time at that job God softened my heart toward this leader. He made it to where my last two or three months, we had the same shift, 3pm to 11pm. By the time 8pm rolled around, business had slowed down and I took that as my opportunity to build with her by listening and serving. I found ways to help her with closing the shift and running the nightly reports. Through our late night conversations, I learned she was unsatisfied in life and work. She was only a few years older than me but felt that the new hires were being promoted quicker than her and she felt overlooked. She was also raised in a family that believed in God but she wasn't sure if she still believed. We were able to build a good working relationship towards the end of my time there. This could not have happened if Jesus wasn't the Lord of my life and work. When I prayed for God's love to be displayed through me, I never envisioned being able to reconcile with this formerly difficult leader, let alone serve her. But that's what God told me to do and I did it. In time, I was healed from the bitterness in my heart. Slowly I started to see that the Holy Spirit was nudging me to start conversations that would point to morality and faith.

Ultimately I shared the gospel with her one evening during our shift. She didn't accept Jesus as Lord and Savior but she did hear The Truth. I was just excited to be obedient in engaging her with the gospel. It was not my responsibility to convert her, only the Lord could do that. My responsibility was only to share the story of Jesus and be an example of God's reconciliation. Yes, it was a daunting task but I'm thankful God used a bitter situation to make me a better colleague and ambassador for him. Through this experience God taught me how to be a reconciler.

> *"Do not repay anyone evil for evil. Be careful to do what is right in the eyes of everyone. If it is possible, as far as it depends on you, live at peace with everyone. Do not take revenge, my dear friends, but leave room for God's wrath, for it is written: "It is mine to avenge; I will repay,"*

> *says the Lord. On the contrary: "If your enemy*
> *is hungry, feed him; if he is thirsty, give him*
> *something to drink. In doing this, you will heap*
> *burning coals on his head." Do not be overcome*
> *by evil, but overcome evil with good." -* Romans
> 12:17-21

Conflict resolution according to God's way is simple. Forgive, give it to God and trust him moving forward as you walk in love. C.S Lewis ("Essays on Forgiveness" (1960)) stated, "To be a Christian means to forgive the inexcusable, because God has forgiven the inexcusable in you."

David and Saul had conflict and lots of it! In 1 Samuel 16:14-23, King Saul was first introduced to David when he was tormented by an evil spirit and needed someone from the kingdom to play the lyre to sooth him. David was the best lyre player and was brought to play for Saul. The next thing we know, in 1 Samuel 17, the Philistines had gathered their forces for war against Saul and Israel. The Philistines had a champion named Goliath. He was a giant who taunted Israel. David was visiting the camp of the Israel army bringing food and supplies for the men. He saw Goliath and immediately wanted to take him down. Unfortunately, he was a young man and many of the men serving in the army urged him to stay away. But David went to Saul and asked for permission to take down Goliath, the champion of the Philistine army. After some convincing David got his way and set out to take down Goliath with only a sling and handful of smooth pebbles. With only one use of his sling shot he took down Goliath and killed him, helping the Israel's army to win the battle against the Philistines.

After Saul was made aware of David's victory he became angry especially when the people of Israel went around singing "Saul has slain his thousands, and David his tens of thousands." (1 Samuel 18:7-8) This is where the seed of jealousy was planted in Saul's heart. David continued to do the right thing, serving Saul and even becoming a leader in the army of Israel. There was one evening when David was playing the lyre and an evil spirit came on Saul and he tried to kill David. David was able to get away safely but this was the beginning of many attacks from his leader(1 Samuel 18:10-11). David could have had revenge but chose not to. Even when Saul was in a vulnerable position, David chose to obey God and not kill him. (1 Samuel 24)

There was even a second opportunity to kill Saul as he was sleeping in his camp with his army but David spared his life again. Instead, David took Saul's spear and water jug that lay near his head. The next day David went to Saul's camp to try again and squash their conflict. He showed Saul that he had the opportunity to take revenge and kill him but chose not to, even while Saul continued to hunt David down to kill him.

As you can see David and King Saul were in constant conflict. King Saul tried to kill David for a long time. David had the opportunity to kill Saul twice but he chose to let God avenge him. King Saul was David's boss and David wanted to respect his leadership. Even when David's life was on the line he chose to trust God to save him and walk in love by not taking any opportunity to get back at Saul. David never once showed his anger or spoke disrespectfully to king Saul. David spoke the truth calling Saul out and telling him how he was wrong for persecuting him with no real cause. David didn't hide from their conflict. He pursued reconciliation with Saul by confronting the problem head on. Even when his colleagues reminded him of all the times Saul wronged him David persisted and sought peace.

What we can learn from David's life in this situation is to seek peace to build a bridge to bring about reconciliation. This means if we have an issue with a leader or a peer at work, confront it head on and state the facts. Then choose to remain at peace with God which will guard our hearts from becoming angry with the world around us. The enemy wants us to have a pity party and question why this is happening to us which usually leads to blaming God. But keep faith in God and continuously read his word for comfort and clarity on how to bring reconciliation. Just like David, God will avenge us but we have to stay close to him and not allow our emotions to dictate how we respond. Or worse allow the company we keep to fill our head with ideas on how to seek revenge. It will not work in our favor if we don't trust God to help and align our behavior with his character.

> *"When we Christians behave badly, or fail to behave well, we are making Christianity unbelievable to the outside world."* - C.S Lewis

You Signed Up for A Fight

When we look at scripture, we are warned that we are up against spiritual dark forces in this world. We win against them when we have on the full armor of God and use his word to stand firm against the enemy and his tactics. I recently heard someone say, "If you've accepted Jesus Christ as Lord and Savior, then you signed up for a fight."

> *"Dear friends, do not be surprised at the fiery ordeal that has come on you to test you, as though something strange were happening to you. But rejoice as much as you participate in the sufferings of Christ, so that you may be overjoyed when his glory is revealed. If you are insulted because of the name of Christ, you are blessed, for the Spirit of glory and of God rests on you. If you suffer, it should not be as a murderer or thief or any other kind of criminal, or even as a meddler. However, if you suffer as a Christian, do not be ashamed, but praise God that you bear that name. For it is time for judgment to begin with God's household; and if it begins with us, what will the outcome be for those who do not obey the gospel of God? And, 'If it is hard for the righteous to be saved, what will become of the ungodly and the sinner?' So then, those who suffer according to God's will should commit themselves to their faithful Creator and continue to do good." - 1 Peter 4:12-19*

Peter shows us how we can stand strong through difficult times. The first thing we must do is acknowledge that we know our faith will be tested. The enemy wants us to think that conflict on our job happens at random. But God's word says we do not fight against flesh and blood. We must realize that the enemy will use people or situations at work to attempt to steer our faith away from trusting in God. This can extend to losing faith to believe for our colleague's salvation or anything in their lives that they need God's restorative power for. There is hope though! 1 Peter 4:12 says, "Don't be surprised at the fiery ordeal that has come on you to test you, as though something strange were happening to you." The message version translates this verse to say, "When life [work] gets really difficult don't jump to the conclusion that God isn't on the job." The faster that we acknowledge that difficult times will come on our jobs, the faster we are to embrace Peter's encouragement of standing strong in the midst of them.

Secondly, we learn to resolve conflict God's way by standing firm in difficult times when we have biblically-based convictions. Part of our job as corporate missionaries is to continue to strengthen our foundation by reading God's word and applying what we have learned daily. At our jobs we can spend forty plus hours each week working with people from all walks of life. We need to strengthen our foundation because we will be tested. Also, we often work with people who don't go to church or have a relationship with God. If they don't see Jesus in us, where will they see him? We may be the only representation of God in their lives.

Our biblically-based convictions help us to choose right from wrong. Convictions are when we have a firmly held belief or opinion, especially when it regards what God has called us to do, how he calls us to live and react. Without convictions we would become just like the world, easily persuaded to sin and live a life that is self-absorbed and absent from God. What a scary thought!

So how is it that we lose our convictions in the workplace? From what I've experienced it's because we try to fit in with the culture, especially when we are faced with conflict or difficulty on our job. The thing is, the enemy wants you to think that you're the only person who is going through issues or difficulties with your colleagues. 1 Peter 5:9 tells us to, "standing firm in the faith, because you know that the family of believers throughout the world is undergoing the same kind of suffering." When we realize that we're not alone in this fight we'll be able to stand firm in our faith. By standing firm we'll start to see that God promised to restore us and make us strong, firm and steadfast (1 Peter 5:10). God doesn't leave us high and dry and left alone to resolve workplace conflict on our own. He wants to empower us by sharing what to say firmly, but with love. He wants to give us strength to battle against the enemy's schemes on our job all while never coming out of our Godly character.

Resolving conflict according to God's word is dear to my heart because as I was promoted, I felt spiritually under attack at work. There would be times when I would ask God, "Why can't I seem to have a peaceful work environment?" With each promotion or each new job the amount of conflict and opposition I faced grew. It was as if the enemy was tormenting me, which he was. But God used a man at my church with the gift of prophecy to speak into my life at a very critical time in my career. This man told me things that only God would have known. Through this conversation, God answered all of my questions and confirmed that I was not in the wrong. I wept deeply because I desperately wanted to see lives changed on my job but there was always some strife or discord happening in my department.

God reminded me of my sophomore year in college when he told me that I would be used for his glory in the corporate world. All the pieces spiritually started to make sense. The great opposition that I felt was an attempt from the enemy to make me lose my footing in Christ. The enemy did not like that I was standing firm in my faith and was ready to go to battle, in prayer, for my colleagues. God's peace was my guard and strength. Philippians 4:7 encourages us saying, "And the peace of God, which transcends all understanding, will guard your hearts and your minds in Christ Jesus." This is your anchor when you choose to pray for help, allowing God's peace to guard your thoughts, your emotions and your will. One of the ways we can preach the gospel is by how we handle conflict. Our response to conflict is either life-giving or destructive. Let's choose life!

CHAPTER 3 – PRACTICAL APPLICATION

In this chapter you read biblical examples on how to resolve conflict, which includes being a peacemaker and recognizing that conflict will exist.

Think of a previous workplace conflict. How did you handle it?

_____

_____

_____

_____

Where is there conflict at work now where you can be a minister of reconciliation? What will that require of you?

_____

_____

_____

_____

Now it's time to dig deeper by going to God's word for his advice. His word is life breathing and when you meditate on it you're able to renew your mind, which can oftentimes be clouded by your situation. God's word will help you to think about your situation with his mind. To get started, think about that current work situation you wrote above. How are you being challenged in this workplace conflict? Are you dealing with pride, anger or comparison?

Whatever it is that you find yourself struggling with, find a scripture that will help you to display Christ's character and bring reconciliation. For example, you can search the internet and type in "bible scriptures on comparison" or you can search for scriptures that pertain to what you're dealing with. Once I've clicked search a list of bible scriptures are displayed. You can either click the links or I like to write them down and read them in my printed bible because I like touching book pages.

What are three scriptures that you can meditate on to encourage you in the above situation? Write them out below.

Scripture #1

_____

_____

_____

_____

Scripture #2

_____

_____

_____

_____

Scripture #3

_____

_____

_____

_____

Prayer

God, help me to trust that you have my best interest at heart. The conflict that I am experiencing...(tell God what the situation looks like and tell Him how it makes you feel, be vulnerable). Show me how to overcome evil with good and to stand firm in my faith. Teach me how to be a peacemaker, so that the world will know that I am a child of God. Help me to seek the counsel of your Holy Spirit, so that I may walk in love instead of wallowing in conflict or worse. Thank you for the tools you've already given me to be successful at resolving conflict and being a reconciler according to your word. Thank you for the gift of your word, which is a spiritual sword. As I go throughout each day at work, remind me to put on the full armor of God, so I can withstand any of the schemes that the enemy may try to hurl my way. I trust and love you. Thank you for helping to shape my life and my career for your glory. In Jesus' name, Amen.

Chapter 4:

ENGAGING YOUR COLLEAGUES

No Matter Your Title or Position, We All Have the Same Commission

Positions, titles and power. These are the things that our society strives for and at a point in my life I was too. At 24 years old, I was fortunate to receive a position with great title and power. On my first promotion my boss asked me to spearhead a team that handled all of the marketing assets from creation to execution across our region. Each day I learned how to manage the team's projects and was thankfully mentored by a few individuals in the company. I wanted to prove myself as a leader and do everything right by the business and the people. I also saw the promotion as a way to advance my name within the company, to show I was someone who could turn a failing department into something successful. God was waiting for me to turn and ask him for guidance. He was calling me to trust him. I yielded to his pursuit and dedicated this new position to him. As I yielded my way for his, God gave me a heart for the people and my desire was to make Jesus' name known among my team.

So, a little background about the team I was working with. Everyone was intelligent, gave great ideas and I appreciated that because it challenged me to always think strategically. Each person came from a unique career background but also a unique spiritual background. Some of my colleagues grew up attending church as a child and some were atheist. Part of my new job included having regularly scheduled one-on-one meetings with each person on my team. I started out having them in my office but it felt too structured. I prayed and asked God how I should conduct these meetings moving forward because something had to change. After a while I felt led to schedule the one-on-ones outside as a walking meeting. This new meeting location was a way to build relationships with each person on my team outside of the typical conference room. I learned about their career aspirations, heard new ideas and got to hear their heart on issues that they were facing.

There was a day when I was on a brief walk in the parking lot and noticed one of my colleagues standing by himself around the side of a building smoking a cigarette. I thought to myself, go say hello and see how he is doing. He was surprised that I came over to speak to him. It was probably because until that moment we had only talked about work-related subjects during time that I specifically carved out each week. However, I felt a nudge from the Holy Spirit to ask him how he was adjusting to the new role and more importantly how he was doing in general. This seemingly "small talk" turned into a quick conversation about purpose and peace. He told me he grew up in a rural town and had some understanding of Christianity based on his upbringing. He shared that he didn't believe in religion because he liked to think of himself as a philosopher, someone who was a theorist and a thinker. I can remember standing in that moment and saying to myself, "Wow, God you've known this man all of his life and right here in this moment you knew that he would be talking to me, help me to point him to you."

As we continued to talk, he mentioned not having peace in his life because he wasn't financially stable, he wanted to quit smoking and he wanted to gain enough experience to reach his dream job. Once he finished sharing, I told him that this new role at times could be stressful but I had found the key to eternal peace and it was me putting all my faith and trust in Jesus Christ. I talked about how I was anxious to perform well on this job to be seen as a great leader within the company. But the peace I had from trusting God to orchestrate my steps on the job outweighed all my anxious thoughts. We talked back and forth for a bit and I could tell that he was curious about Jesus and this eternal peace but he didn't understand the full story. I shared with him what Jesus did by taking the punishment we deserved and was crucified on a cross, dying the death we as sinners should have died but then rose again on the third day proving that he was the son of God and whoever believes (puts their faith in him) would be reconciled with God and will have eternal life. But the story didn't stop there because I knew this precious moment may not come again. At the end of our talk, I told him Jesus Christ died so we could live life abundantly on this earth not just for life after death but for now too. I could tell this was all foreign to him but I saw a seed planted for God's kingdom.

Over time we developed a strong working relationship and through it God gave me a platform to continue to speak the truth of the gospel to him. He even accepted an invitation to attend a lifegroup at my home. An atheist attending a bible study. I was shocked that he came. He even participated by volunteering to read a scripture. Mind blown. Shortly after sharing the gospel with him and seeing how open he was to attending a lifegroup, I figured I had a short window of time to invite him to church. So I extended the invite and he came! Although he arrived at the very end of service, my husband and I were able to introduce him to our pastor and some of our friends. I believe this colleague began to experience the love of God for the first time. A seed was planted. He eventually moved back to his hometown. From time to time, I would call or text to follow up but we eventually lost touch. I still pray for him.

Everyday I took a few minutes to pray in my office. During this time God would begin to reveal words of knowledge for each person on my team. He once showed me that a colleague was on the verge of poverty. After praying how to approach them, God gave me the exact words I needed to say to encourage her along with offering to give her rides wherever she needed. She and her boyfriend were trying to balance dropping off their kid to daycare and making it on time for work with one car. Although I shared my personal testimony with her, I never felt as if it made an impact, that is until I became the literal hands and feet of Jesus by giving her rides. Our rides together gave me such joy knowing that I was serving her and her family as I know Jesus would. As I remember these moments today, God used my promotion, that new position, as a platform to make His name known and bring truth to my team. The key to His plan, as it often is, was having a willing person ready and available to share the truth with people who thought they didn't need God. Although, this example involves sharing the gospel after receiving a promotion, God doesn't care about your position or title. He only requires that you are ready and available to follow His lead to reach your colleagues.

Romans 10:13-17 says, "for everyone who calls on the name of the Lord will be saved. How, then, can they call on the one they have not believed in? And how can they believe in the one of whom they have not heard? And how can they hear without someone preaching to them? And how can anyone preach unless they are sent? As it is written: "How beautiful are the feet of those who bring good news!"

Jesus commanded those who follow him in Matthew 28:18-20 to make disciples to the ends of the earth. This is great however international trips are not always possible or are infrequent. What is possible is for you to share the gospel to the ends of your job. And let me be clear, yes, go on mission trips and yes, they can be international but do not neglect the fact that when we drive to work each day, this becomes our daily and practical show of obedience to Christ's command in Matthew 28:18-20. This is the great commission.

As the body of Christ, we get the privilege to be his hands and feet by sharing this great news which brings eternal life, salvation, justification, sanctification, and so many other wonderful promises from God. Now at this point, your heart may be beating fast and your mind may be giving you every reason why you should not go and share the gospel with your colleagues. As we discussed earlier, the Holy Spirit will guide and counsel you in each moment if you let Him. Paul writes in Romans 10:13 "... everyone who calls on the name of the Lord will be saved." But what must occur for someone to call on the name of the Lord? Someone must first be sent to proclaim the good news of the gospel, and then listeners must pay attention and believe.

So where does that leave you in the midst of God's great commission? Maybe you've tried to share the gospel with a colleague and were rejected. Did you give yourself a big pep talk only to lose that momentum and abort your mission because of fear? Or maybe you've made up your mind that you are not ready spiritually because you need to work on your relationship with God. Then you'll be equipped to do something like share the gospel with your colleagues.

Listen, I've been able to answer yes to both of these questions at some point in my walk with Christ. There have been times when the Holy Spirit wanted to speak through me to encourage colleagues who were spilling their heart out. But I kept my mouth shut because of fear. Also, when I started walking with God I felt like I had a long to-do list of things that would make me qualified to share the gospel. What I've learned is the only qualification is to be available and obedient to follow God's lead. We have to rely on his strength and power not our own. The disappointment I felt when I chickened out led to my change and it fueled me to trust the Holy Spirit as a guide. The next time I was presented with an opportunity, I took it. I had to let go of my fear of having to say things perfectly. God doesn't care about your title or position at work, you do. He has qualified you no matter your position. With an obedient heart to follow his commission, he is well pleased.

Before long another opportunity presented itself. This time on an out of town business trip in Palm Beach, FL. The organization that I worked for sponsored an annual conference and we drove down as a team. We had plans to take tennis lessons, network and relax by the pool but God had a different agenda.

On the first day I knew God was calling me to be bold for him on this trip. My colleagues and I checked into the hotel and had planned to meet at the pool for lunch. I went down to the pool and was met by one of my colleagues. She held a senior role within the organization. I felt a little out of place talking to her because her position was much higher than mine. After a few minutes of waiting we realized that our other colleagues weren't going to make the trip down because of the nearby bad weather that was traveling our way. I believe this was God-designed timing because it gave us a chance to connect. Other than a few small projects our previous interactions were limited but I saw an opportunity to build a relationship. Our small talk turned into work talk, which then turned into a conversation about purpose. I shared with her that I was a few weeks away from my wedding day and how excited I was for the big day. She asked if we had lived together before marriage. I replied no, and she asked why. I told her that we had committed ourselves to God first and wanted to honor him with our relationship. Although not perfect we chose to walk together and stay accountable to our spiritual family.

This seemingly casual conversation was the catalyst that helped me share the gospel. Shortly after sharing the gospel the conversation died down but she thanked me for being transparent. We worked in two different states so we didn't communicate very often at work. I never got a chance to truly follow up on the deeper things that we discussed but I felt like God used me at that time to encourage her and share a message of hope.

Throughout that weekend God allowed me to see that my colleagues were thirsty for truth and sound wisdom. I couldn't help but think to myself 'why me God' as I was the youngest person on the trip. As I look back on that time, I now realize that I was walking in God's will for my life. He allowed his Holy Spirit to give me the words to say. All my past failures were used as an encouragement of hope as I shared how I came to realize that Jesus' life, death and resurrection was the turning point for a life of freedom.

Having Faith is the First Step in Engaging Your Colleagues

Hebrews 11:1 NIV states, "Faith is the assurance of things hoped for and the confidence for things not seen."

What does it look like to have faith for your colleagues? Taking from the scripture in Hebrews we can equate that in all things God wants us to have faith for things hoped for and have confidence for the things not seen. In our work lives, we can have faith for our colleague's salvation, breakthrough or a deeper understanding of God's word, especially if they are already believers. Practically, having faith for our colleagues can include praying for them in our quiet time with the Lord, speaking life-giving words over them and loving them exactly where they are at.

Having Faith and Praying for Your Colleagues

First, pray that God would remove Satan's blinding influence. 2 Corinthians 4:4 says, "The god of this age has blinded the minds of unbelievers, so that they cannot see the light of the gospel that displays the glory of Christ, who is the image of God." The bible also teaches us that the world we live in is ruled by the enemy and his dark spiritual forces. Whether our unbelieving colleagues know it or not, they have been blinded towards the gospel by the enemy. Part of our jobs as corporate missionaries is to pray against this and ask God to open their spiritual eyes to see him clearly.

After we've prayed for their spiritual eyes to be opened, we pray that God would open their hearts to believe the gospel. God is the only one with the power to change someone's heart. God initiates by touching their hearts and then they are left to respond. (Acts 16:14 NIV)

Finally, our prayer is that our colleagues come to Christ. Christ is the only way to salvation. Jesus stated, "I am the way, and the truth and the life. No one comes to the Father except through me..." John 14:6. Our prayers are powerful! Try praying this over a few of your colleagues and watch God work! I prayed these prayers countless times and watched God reveal himself to one colleague who I wasn't even sure would come around. She was hard to teach because she had so many questions that I started to believe I wasn't equipped to share the gospel with her. But I prayed to God to help her understand and went home to research answers. After a few weeks, God answered my prayers. He opened her heart to receive His truth. Even though she didn't have the answers to all of her questions she still took a leap of faith and believed. God used that experience to show me that I needed to continue having faith. After leading her to Christ, I also had the privilege of discipling and teaching her bible foundations. I watched how God used my prayers to reveal more of himself and gave her a heart of flesh, removing her heart of stone. Our prayers are powerful and God uses us to fight spiritually against the enemy's forces that keep so many of our colleagues bound as slaves to sin.

So, are you ready to go before the throne of God on behalf of your colleagues? In the new testament, Paul knelt to pray for the gentiles all while being imprisoned and in chains. His story picks up in Ephesians 3:14-19. We too can have faith like Paul who, in his occupation as an Apostle, prayed for the Ephesians.

He prayed, "For this reason, I kneel before the Father, from whom every family in heaven and on earth derives its name. I pray that out of his glorious riches he may strengthen you with power through his Spirit in your inner being, so that Christ may dwell in your hearts through faith. And I pray that you, being rooted and established in love, may have power, together with all the Lord's holy people, to grasp how wide and long and high and deep is the love of Christ, and to know this love that surpasses knowledge—that you may be filled to the measure of all the fullness of God. Now to him who is able to do immeasurably more than all we ask or imagine, according to his power that is at work within us, to him be glory in the church and in Christ Jesus throughout all generations, forever and ever! Amen."

I encourage you to take this scripture and pray it aloud adding in your colleague's name. I've provided a template below.

Father, I kneel before you, from whom every family in heaven and on earth derives its name. I pray for *insert name* that she/he will come to know Jesus Christ as her/his Lord and Savior and that out of your glorious riches they may be strengthened with your power through your Holy Spirit in their inner being. I pray that Christ may dwell in *insert name* heart through faith and that they, being rooted and established in love, may have power, together with all the Lord's holy people. That she/he may grasp how wide and long and high and deep is the love of Christ, and to know this love that surpasses knowledge—that they may be filled to the measure of all the fullness of God. I know you are able to do immeasurably more than all I can ask or imagine, according to your power that is at work within us. I will glorify your name forever and ever! In Jesus' name, Amen."

God's promise to us is "whatever we ask in prayer, we will receive, if we have faith." (Matthew 21:22)

Do you have faith for your colleagues?

Having Faith and Speaking Words of Life

The second part of having faith when engaging our colleague's is speaking life. Words can be powerful. Proverbs 18:25 NIV says, "The tongue has the power of life and death, and those who love it will eat its fruit." What type of words do you speak over your colleagues? Have you sown words of encouragement or the opposite? Ephesians 4:29 (NIV) says, "Do not let any unwholesome talk come out of your mouths, but only what is helpful for building others up according to their needs, that it may benefit those who listen." The words we choose to describe our colleagues are seeds that will eventually produce fruit. It all depends on the type of crop you've sown to determine what type of fruit will grow.

Practically, speaking life starts with your everyday conversations. For example, you've been praying for a colleague, but they can't seem to grasp a strategic concept at work or they're in a season of complaining. We may catch ourselves saying, "they are such a complainer" or "they just can't understand this concept." Without even thinking we've spoken words of death. Not literal death but death, nonetheless. So, you shouldn't be surprised when they never understand that concept or if they're complaining grows worse because you've labeled them as such. Our words have power.

I'm sure we've all found ourselves saying something negative about a colleague either directly or indirectly. Well, be encouraged because this is not a shame on you section but if the Holy Spirit convicts you, you might want to follow whatever he's telling you.

God gives us the ability through his Holy Spirit to have our minds renewed. This benefit comes only after we accept Christ as Lord over our lives and it helps us to think his thoughts as we immerse ourselves in His Word. Romans 12:2 (NIV) confirms this by saying, "Do not conform to the pattern of this world, but be transformed by the renewing of your mind. Then you will be able to test and approve what God's will is—his good, pleasing and perfect will."

Speaking life and having our minds renewed is a process not a single event. It is a spiritual transformation where the Holy Spirit works in us to have the mind of Christ so we can think and speak His words. Philippians 4:8 (NIV) says, "Finally, brothers and sisters, whatever is true, whatever is noble, whatever is right, whatever is pure, whatever is lovely, whatever is admirable—if anything is excellent or praiseworthy—think about such things."

Half the battle is won in our minds. If we are thinking with the mind of Christ for our colleagues, we'll see the harvest that we prayed for. What can you think of or say that will speak life over your colleagues this week?

Having Faith and Love

Lastly, having faith for your colleagues must be rooted in love. 1 John 4:19 says, "We love because He first loved us." Even on our worst days when we are the ones who look like we need Jesus all over again, God still loves us. This tenderness and heartfelt love should be displayed even in our jobs. This does not mean we become passive towards our corporate goals but we get to display love and compassion where it's needed the most.

Practically we find our example of what love looks like in 1 Corinthians 13:4-8, "Love is patient and kind; love does not envy or boast; it is not arrogant or rude. It does not insist on its own way; it is not irritable or resentful; it does not rejoice at wrongdoing, but rejoices with the truth. Love bears all things, believes all things, hopes all things, endures all things. Love never ends. As for prophecies, they will pass away; as for tongues, they will cease; as for knowledge, it will pass away."

Love is patient and kind – Romans 2:4 says, "...God's kindness is intended to lead us to repentance." If we align ourselves with loving our colleagues like Christ, we may very well see the power of God's kindness and patience through us lead them to salvation.

Love does not envy or boast – God intends for us to be content in him. What Paul means is that if you lack assurance or contentment, you may find yourself experiencing jealousy in your heart. This could play out if you see God bless a colleague that you've been praying for and they get more favor than you. As a child of God, the enemy wants to keep you stuck from loving your colleagues by whispering these types of ideas. Boasting is simply a technique that we use to bring glory to ourselves. But we exemplify God's love when we rely on him commending us, rather than us seeking out praise. This is learned through discipline and our colleagues who watch from afar will see us choose God's way, which can be a witness to them as well.

Love does not insist on its own way. It is not irritable or resentful. Simply put, don't be selfish and rude.

Overall, God's love is powerful and practical when we choose to operate his way. He wants the very things we desire for our colleagues, for them to know him and live for him.

Being Faithful

Recently I had been praying for God to open one of colleagues' eyes to see him and her need for a savior. In the midst of praying, I also made a commitment to God that I would engage in conversation with her daily. Whether it be me stopping by her office to say hello or setting up time to eat together. I made my interactions with her a priority. That's what being faithful is all about. It's walking in obedience to what God has asked us to do, not just sometimes but every day.

Luke 16:10 says, "Whoever can be trusted with very little can also be trusted with much, and whoever is dishonest with very little will also be dishonest with much."

Faithfulness is not determined by the quantity entrusted but by the character of the person who uses it. God is looking for men and women who are convinced that being faithful to share the gospel will lead to seeing their colleagues accept Jesus as Lord and Savior one day. We work with our colleagues 40, 50, sometimes 60 hours a week and for some of us we've been on our jobs for 5, 10, 15 years. It's not a lack of time to engage them but a lack of heart to believe God for the strength to run this long-distance race. Remember, being faithful to engage our colleagues means we rely on God's spirit not our own power or might.

Chapter 4 – Practical Application

This chapter focused on a central message, activating your faith to believe God will reveal himself to your colleagues. We read this scripture earlier but I find it appropriate to read it again. Hebrews 11:1 encourages us by saying, "Faith is the assurance of things hoped for and the confidence for things not seen."

Take a minute to think about this. Does your faith show that you are assured of things hoped for (your colleagues coming to know and accept Jesus as their Lord and Savior)? Are you truly confident about these things that are not seen? However you answered, God wants to encourage you to keep believing for your colleagues salvation and to keep your faith rooted in him.

List the names of colleagues (past or present) who you are believing to come into a relationship with Jesus Christ.

a. _____

b. _____

c. _____

d. _____

e. _____

Now, I love organization. So, we're going to organize our prayers of faith for each individual listed above.

Name	Having faith through prayer.	Having faith and speaking words of life.	Having faith and showing love.
	*Based on your relationship with each person, what are some specific prayer points that you can pray over their life. Bonus points if you can find a scripture that correlates with your prayer strategy.	*Based on your relationship with each person, what are some specific ways you can encourage them that may open a door for you to share the gospel. (Job, family, marriage, children, finances, etc.)	*Taking from 1 Corinthians 13:1-11, how can you show God's love towards each person on your list.
Example: Suzan W.	*- Deals with anxiety (Phil 4:13)* *- Went to church as a kid, no belief in God as an adult (Acts 26:18)* *- Teenage children are rebelling and being disobedient to follow instructions.*	*- Ask open ended questions about the source of her peace? And share bite size pieces of your testimony in this area (remember: Make Jesus the Hero of the story!)* *- Write words of encouragement that will encourage her work, family, etc.*	*- Be present, listen to understand and show patience when she is venting or showing anxiety.* *- Invite Susan to share lunch or dinner (with you and/or with both families)*

A			
B			
C			

D			
E			

Chapter 5:

TREASURE IN THE WORKPLACE

In the parable of the "rich fool" we see two brothers and one inheritance. It starts in Luke 12, where we read that one of the brothers asked Jesus to tell the other brother to share the inheritance with him. But Jesus doesn't address the rich fool's question. Instead he deals straight with the heart, saying in verse 15, "Beware! Guard against every kind of greed. Life is not measured by how much you own." Now why would Jesus go on to say a thing like that? Couldn't he have told the brothers to split the inheritance? Jesus' reply was a dart that landed dead center on the condition of the rich fool's heart. What we can gather from this parable is that the rich fool was stressed out over his father's inheritance because he had built his life's value on it. The fact that he was passive aggressive towards his brother (waited until there was a large crowd to address him about the inheritance) proves that this issue was a trigger.

But Jesus' gentle reply spoke to the fact that his problem was trying to draw value from a temporary treasure. His treasure or rather his value was under attack and he didn't know how to secure it. But as we later read Jesus provides a proposition for the rich fool to base his treasure in heaven where it cannot be destroyed. Jesus wanted to give him new treasure and he wants to give you the same. Think about this. Do you find yourself stressed at work over things that do not matter in eternity? Like getting aggravated when a colleague walks by but didn't greet you, or your boss assigns you to train the intern? There are many scenarios to draw from but if you struggle with any anger or discontentment in the workplace, especially when your position or tenure is insulted, you may be suffering from a distressed treasure, just like the rich fool.

To be honest, I suffered from this same type of distress. There were times when I would be so infuriated because of something my colleagues did, something they said or because I wasn't included in a special project. God showed me my discontentment. I was so fixated on success in my work instead of rooting my success in Him. I wish I could go back and tell my younger self to calm down and store up treasure in heaven instead of chasing power, recognition, popularity and promotion. I was so stuck. The issue wasn't in the things that I aspired to be or the things I wanted to have. It was that my heart wasn't submitted to the process of building spiritual wealth. My heart desired earthly treasures more than it desired heavenly treasures. I formulated a plan that equaled contentment based on what I had at work. Wrong! Wrong! Wrong! I was so misled. God, though, used my spiritual family to help me see that all the glory belongs to God. If I wasn't trying to use the power or recognition I received to make Him known amongst my colleagues, then I would be chasing a fleeting dream that never amounted to the spiritual fullness I could have.

Matthew 6:19-21 says, "Do not lay up for yourselves treasures on earth, where moth and rust destroy and where thieves break in and steal, but lay up for yourselves treasures in heaven, where neither moth nor rust destroys and where thieves do not break in and steal. For where your treasure is, there your heart will be also." In my opinion Matthew Henry (a), a commentator, breaks this passage down the best, saying, "...Therefore Christ, having warned us against coveting the praise of men, proceeds next to warn us against coveting the wealth of the world; in this also we must take heed, lest we be as the hypocrites are, and do as they do: the fundamental error that they are guilty of is, that they choose the world for their reward."

Ouch! That still hurts to read because it can be so easy to allow our work routine and everyday life to become wrapped up in what we can get here and now. God has treasure for us in Heaven, where it cannot be destroyed or stolen. Unlike the fleeting treasures of our success at work.

Treasurable Moments

We've just learned that we should store up our treasure in Heaven. But how do you handle a huge win at work that provides an unexpected bonus or promotion? What about receiving praise from your spiritual family for sharing the gospel with others? We can cherish these moments because they are a glimpse of what is to come. I like to call these treasurable moments in light of eternity. In this life we will receive praise for the good works that we do. However, earthly praise is temporary and fleeting. God doesn't want us to get conceited though, thinking more highly of ourselves than we ought. He wants us to feel encouraged and excited about telling our colleagues about him. But when you get that pat on the back or whether you get a huge win at work, look at it as a deposit for the real moment when you get to stand before the Lord and hear, "Well done my good and faithful servant" (Matthew 25:21). These treasurable moments in light of eternity should always point us back to Him.

Ecclesiastes 3:11 says, "...He has also set eternity in the human heart." This innate awareness that there is something more than what we experience on this earth has been placed by God in our hearts. For believers this awareness of eternity comes with the hope that we will one day experience the glory of the Lord and bask in His presence. That is our eternal treasurable moment.

CHAPTER 5 - PRACTICAL APPLICATION

Take some time to reflect on all of the things that God has blessed you with. List them out and thank God for each of them.

_____

_____

_____

_____

Think of ways you can give God the glory using the things that he has blessed you with. If you need ideas, ask God, he's the best advisor.

_____

_____

_____

_____

Let us pray...

Father, when I am blessed with earthly treasures help me to stay humble. Remind me through your Holy Spirit that I should store up treasures in heaven where they are eternal and never fleeting. Show me how to use my earthly treasures to bring you glory on my job. Give me guidance on how to live a humble life that isn't defined by the stuff you give me while on this earth. Part of that is renewing my mind daily by meditating on your word day and night. I want to please you by the way I live my life and by living up to the calling you have given me. Help me each day and show me how. In Jesus' name. Amen.

Corporate Missionary is a movement that exists to equip and empower believers to share the gospel at work. We want to honor God by establishing Christians in all seasons of their career in a strong biblical foundation.

We offer resources for personal or group use. Our courses are for people at all stages of their working lives.

For more information about Corporate Missionary and it's work around the world, please visit our website and social media.

Website: www.corporatemissionary.org

Instagram: @corporatemissionary

LinkedIn: www.linkedin.com/ company/corporate-missionary

NOTES

NOTES

NOTES

NOTES

NOTES

NOTES

NOTES

NOTES

NOTES

NOTES

NOTES

NOTES

NOTES

NOTES

NOTES

NOTES

NOTES